My Friend Daniel Doesn't Talk

Sharon L. Longo
Illustrated by Jane Bottomley

 Routledge
Taylor & Francis Group

LONDON AND NEW YORK

D1465244

First published 2006 by Speechmark Publishing Ltd.

Published 2017 by Routledge

2 Park Square, Milton Park, Abingdon, Oxon OX14 4RN

711 Third Avenue, New York, NY 10017, USA

Routledge is an imprint of the Taylor & Francis Group, an informa business

British Library Cataloguing in Publication Data
Longo, Sharon
        My friend Daniel doesn't talk
        1. Mutism, Elective - Juvenile fiction 2. Bashfulness in children - Juvenile
        fiction 3. Friendship - Juvenile fiction 4. Children with social disabilities -
        Education (Elementary) 5. Children's stories
        I. Title II. Bottomley, Jane
        823.9'2[J]

ISBN 9780863885624 (pbk)

To Brian, for your strength and determination –
One day the words will come.

Daniel was the new kid in our class. That first day he played with his shirt collar while his mother talked to our teacher, and his face was frozen, as if he was scared and sad at the same time. He hardly even nodded when Miss Antonio asked him a question.

I always talk too much. Mom says I could be the mayor one day. My teachers say I need to settle down a bit.

'Hi, my name's Ryan. What's yours?'

Daniel just looked down at the floor and then walked away.

'What's wrong with him?' Carlos asked, pointing and making a face.

'Shy, I guess,' I said.

Daniel didn't say anything the rest of the day.

The next day I asked Daniel if he wanted to be my reading partner. He nodded, but then I did all of the reading. I knew he could read because he shook his head when I pronounced the word choir with a 'ch' sound, like in the word chair. He did the same thing while we were adding, nodding when I gave the right answer, and holding up his fingers to correct me when I was wrong.

'Come on, Daniel, say something to me,' I said quietly at lunchtime, but Daniel seemed to get upset, crumpling up his sandwich in the plastic wrapping and shoving it in his lunchbox. I didn't say much after that.

I asked my mom about him because she talked to Daniel's mom.

'Daniel is afraid to talk in school,' she told me.

I'm afraid of the dark sometimes! Being afraid to talk … that would be awful!

'How could someone feel that afraid in school?'
Ben asked the next day, after I explained to some
of the kids about Daniel.

'He's just weird,' Jonathon said, 'the way he
points and nods. Maybe he's an alien.'

Jonathon loves to daydream about aliens and
space creatures, but he doesn't think much about
other people's feelings. He ran off to try and join
in with Carlos and some other kids.

I tried to answer Ben's question, and the other kids listened.

'My mom said some kids are so scared to talk that their words can't come out. She said we should just leave Daniel alone and then one day he might talk.'

Jessica wrinkled her nose the way she does when she sees a fluffy little rabbit or someone's baby sister.

'I think Daniel is so cute! I'm going to be extra nice to him so he'll talk to me one day!' She clapped her hands excitedly.

'Oh great,' I said, picturing Jessica talking baby talk to Daniel and trying to act like his mom.

That afternoon, Daniel chose me to be his partner in class again, and he even smiled on the playground!

Mom said Daniel could come over after school one day, and when he finally did, I couldn't believe it when he whispered to me when we were alone!

'This is a cool racecar set,' Daniel said softly.

I could have said, 'Wow, you talked!' but mom says we shouldn't make a big deal when Daniel speaks. That would just make him feel more upset.

After a while, Daniel was talking out loud to me. We talked about our favorite teams and TV shows. We had a lot of fun together!

Daniel didn't say anything when Mom came into the room to tell him it was time to go home.

The next day Daniel only nodded at me in school. At first I felt bad when he didn't talk to me in school, as if he wasn't really my friend. But we play together a lot now, and he talks to me all the time. Not in school, though.

In class, Miss Antonio lets me go with Daniel if he has to run an errand or go to the nurse. She says I can be his voice. Sometimes talking too much is good!

Mom says Daniel is getting some help, and one day he'll be able to talk to me in school. I hope so. Then the other kids can see what he's really like.

For now, it's ok that my friend Daniel doesn't talk. I'll just keep helping him until he can.

Guide for Parents and Teachers

This book is intended to educate all children so they may understand that there are others, like Daniel, who are so 'shy' or socially anxious that they are unable to talk to others. It is also meant to be an example of how they can reach out to these children and be a good friend. Even if a child never meets another child with selective mutism, the theme of reaching out to someone who is 'different' or who is hurting in some way is a universal one, one that we need to teach all children.

For teachers who are trying to understand selective mutism, as well as trying to explain this to their students, this is an invaluable tool. However, this book should never be read to the class while the child with selective mutism is present or without their permission.

It is important for teachers and others who interact with the child to understand that expecting speech from a child with selective mutism will only increase the anxiety. Determining which stage of communication the child is at and allowing the child to rate their own anxiety level in different settings will help anyone who works with the child to understand which steps are necessary to move toward verbal communication. Communication scales vary but usually go from non-communication (verbal and nonverbal), to nonverbal communication (nodding, writing answers, pointing), to responding with sounds, to steps leading up to speech with a keyworker or verbal intermediary, which increases to include more people and varied places. Anxiety scales also vary and may include numbers from zero to five, with zero being very easy and five being very difficult, or pictures such as a big smile, denoting lower anxiety, to a worried face, denoting higher anxiety.

All of this takes time and a lot of small steps before verbalization actually occurs. Patience is key. The earlier selective mutism is diagnosed and treated, the easier the transition from non-communication to verbal communication will be.

For parents of a child with selective mutism, this book is intended to give hope that there is someone like Ryan out there who will be a kind and understanding friend to your child. For parents whose children attend class with a child who is extremely shy or suffering from selective mutism, perhaps your child could be that friend! It is important for parents to realize that getting help for their child in the setting where anxiety is most prevalent, namely school, is necessary in order to overcome this.

Lastly, for the child who has selective mutism, this book may initially arouse negative emotions, reminding them of the fact that they are, in fact, unable to speak in school. However, having this book on hand during their recovery allows the child to read the book in its entirety or to skim only a few pages, while coming back to the topic as they begin to feel more comfortable. The choice is theirs!

Suggested reading

Johnson M & Wintgens A, 2001, *The Selective Mutism Resource Manual*, Speechmark Publishing, Bicester.

Shipon-Blum E, 2003, *The Ideal Classroom Setting for the Selectively Mute Child*, Self-published.

Kervatt, Gail, 1999, *The Silence Within*, Self-published.

Other organizations

SMIRA (Selective Mutism Information and Research Association), 1 Ridgeway Road, Leicester, LE2 3LH, UK.

SMG-CAN (Selective Mutism Group-Childhood Anxiety Network), www.selectivemutism.org

The Selective Mutism Foundation Inc, PO Box 13133, Sissonville, WV 25360-0133, USA

Freedom from Fear, 308 Seaview Ave, Staten Island, New York 10305 USA Phone: (718) 351-1717, fff@aol.com

ASHA (American Speech-Language-Hearing Association), www.asha.org

About the author

Sharon Longo is a teacher and writer, married with three children, one with selective mutism.

    She has written and published numerous articles on selective mutism and has won several awards for her work.